Other Possible Lives

Other books by Chrissy Kolaya

Any Anxious Body: poems

Charmed Particles: a novel

OTHER POSSIBLE LIVES

CHRISSY KOLAYA

Broadstone

Library of Congress Control Number 2019938697

ISBN 978-1-937968-56-4

Text Design by Stephanie Potter

Cover Design by Larry W. Moore
Cover artwork "Southern Light" by Michael Eble,
used by permission

Broadstone Books
An Imprint of
Broadstone Media LLC
418 Ann Street
Frankfort, KY 40601-1929
BroadstoneBooks.com

For Brook, Parker, and Ellis:

my best possible life

CONTENTS

I. THE HOUSE SITTERS

THE HOUSE SITTERS

i.

They play at being retired or married, spend the night in a feather-bed four feet off the floor, where they make love, where she crawls beneath the covers and the bed creaks with no one to hear it.

That afternoon, she floated in circles in the pool, music drifting out over the deck.

At dusk, the couples arrive. Some of them married. Some will be years from now. Some will leave each other. It's easy to imagine—

—this house as hers, this man as hers, but she knows it's unlikely she'll end up this way and happy.

ii.

She touches the photographs—the woman and her sons—a book left open on a nightstand, fat tubes of creams and ointments in the bathroom drawers. Prescription bottles stacked in the guest bath. *The second husband's dying of cancer*, he had told her the first night there.

She reads the note left behind—vet's number, plumber's—traces the woman's long cursive with her fingertip.

At night the house sitters climb the stairs, the dogs slumbering by the pool, where water laps the terra cotta.

iii.

The night before in their own house, with gaps between the floorboards, whose walls creak like a sad animal, fireflies come in through the air conditioner, out of the humidity and into the cold where the house sitters sometimes sleep like strangers, sometimes sleep like children, where she watches him at first dawn, follows the lines of his arms, jaw, feels lucky.

That night they had made love just before sleep, fireflies circling overhead in the dark. He moved over her, then stopped.

"There," he said, looking down, indicating the spot where her nipple met the mattress, the yellow-green glow just beside the aureole, blinking on and off.

She holds her breath, afraid they'll crush it, this luminescent beetle.

iv.

In the afternoon he reads a novel in the living room, house chilled with the air conditioning, back door open for the dogs to come and go—she dreams of this, and when she wakes, he stands in the doorway, a silhouette.

Looks out at her, shading his eyes, and says something about the temperature that means he might love her, at least for the evening.

v.

One morning they watch a deer creep out of its hiding place, the lab bounding off, the wolfhound galumphing after her in his strange sideways canter, a misguided belief he might catch something so quick.

vi.

She waits up for him, flips the channels of the big-screen t.v. The house, lit from within, glows out against the panes of the window.

Outside, the dogs howl at the purpled sky they smell on the horizon.

vii.

After the argument, she ducks out, tiptoes through the house of strangers where he sleeps with his back to her, hands to himself. So that the next morning, looking all over, he is, as he later tells her, distraught. And she pictures old women, inconsolable.

viii.

The scale's needle hovers like an insect between one weight and another. She's an intruder in this other woman's bathroom, her reflection in the mirror—foreign, and she's half-afraid she might leave some trace of her behind.

The house—immaculate, no signs of such upheaval: how this woman had left one husband for another, how her belly had swelled first for one son, then another.

She thinks of how this summer, hers is a dream life, borrowed.

ix.

The people are home now, rooms filled with their rightful owners. In the children's rooms favorite toys are found, beds turned down. The dog cavorts in his clumsy way, the only one there to welcome them home.

The house sitters have returned to their own house, whose floors slant, whose doors creak in gentle breezes.

They will fall back in love, and a while later fall out of it. Will leave each other one afternoon—it's easy to imagine.

And though it wasn't, when they remember, they'll think of this house as theirs, their lapped terra cotta, clumsy Wolfhound, playing at love.

II. GEOGRAPHICA

DRIVING AT NIGHT

Across the highway darts a fox,
eyes reflected in the headlights
of the lone approaching car.

A winding road so dark
it feels as though
we might tumble off the earth
as we speed forward,
round curves where
at any moment
a deer might startle,
silvery flank
lit by headlights,
then gone
in an instant,
disappearing
back into woods
rising up
on either side of the car.

Trucks along the shoulder
cradle sleepers stretched out in cabs
littered with empty soda bottles, bags of chips.

The smooth system of interstate highways—
long slender fingers
gathering the states together
in the darkness.

ISLE AU HAUT

Parker at ninety-six
steps gingerly into the boat,
settles into a seat on the deck
where the sea air
ruffles his hair.

The high island, he says
indicating the land
rising out of the water.

Seals sunning themselves on a rock
watch as the boat motors past.

Parker prefers a sail,
but for today's purpose,
this will do.

At the dock
he's helped from the boat,
settled into a rusty jeep
waiting by the water's edge.

Over the rough road
though his eyesight is nearly gone,
he knows they pass the store
stocked for the summer people with
caviar and duck confit,
past the P.O.
open 9-11 a.m.,
then to the house
where he'll be fed corn chowder
and blueberry pie.

His hosts and the young people
set out on a tour of the island.
Parker stays behind
resting on a couch along a wall of windows
looking out over a field of wildflowers
and beyond them,
the sea.

DEAR BOAT,

Please rock gently in the water
tethered to an orange and green-
striped buoy. Please

watch as the waves
rush against the shoreline, shush,
shush, shush, then

away. Fill
with laughing children,
shouting at the shoreline, yellow

boat, blue boat. Gather
the salty breeze against your hull,
sea air,
dogs running the shore.
Around you

wraps the Cape,
arms encircling,
drawing you close. Here

Here. Waves
run over and in all at once,
gulls overhead,

your prow
dipping deep into wave.
You say—*geography,*

desire. Don't think I'm speaking
in some kind of code
you're meant to figure out.

How to Leave Behind

After decades of moving every year
my mother knew the art
of leaving people behind.

She said the way to do it was
to look at a photo of them.
Look at it until their faces
melt away into lines,
until words like *brother* fall away

and swirl around the shape that's left.
To focus on the mouth,
then the eyes,
then the arms and legs as if they all belonged
to different people.

And they did. Soon
you'd barely recognize the person.
You'd barely be able
to put their face back together after that.
Francesca falls away. Then Dan and Vern

and Ray. Here's some woman from your wedding—
a shirt, a sleeve,
a name.
The dress falls away,

the pose in the photo.
Your arm around some brother.
Say it over again—
JayJayJay
and he is only a sound
a line
a swirling.

Fall, On Its Way In

Outside, the wind kicks up a little storm in the driveway—

swirling leaves whose colors
have begun to change,
going brittle around the edges, the sky
the pink sort of grey that means soon
the weather will be changing,

sun falling by five o'clock.

By this time of year
bees have abandoned their hives.
I don't know where they go—
I don't think about them
all winter—my take
on the natural sciences
is dubious.

The trees shift with the wind—
branches pulling,
matted together, struggling
against this cooperative
of treeness. The smell of perfume
on the sleeve of your jacket—

The trees speak,
whispering
the same way
they have for years.

BLIZZARD, COLLEGE TOWN

Students walk down the middle of the street,
sidewalks abandoned—
Pompei under the ash—

lost cities under the snow. The world turns white
for the winter. Two inches
in an hour,

and the men of Minnesota
stand by their windows and watch,
waiting until it's exhausted itself
before beginning to dig out.

The morning will bloom
with the sound of snowblowers coming to life.
For now,
the flakes come down
like rain in slow motion.

FLIGHT

Cranes descend,
legs dangling,
wings spread,
like jumpers from a building.

From above,
the earth neatly divided:
rice field,
soy field,
village,
ocean.

What causes the waves?
he asks.
*The beating
of birds' wings.*

The gannet shifts
from wide parenthesis
to slim arrow,
exclamation point
dropping into the sea.

Here they float
like white clouds.
Here
frozen earth
comes down around them.
Black sparrows
swarm together
and apart,
a secret liquid
taking shape.

Slim sailboat in the distance.
One of their kind—
white crane
on the water.

The goose
picks its way
down the railroad tracks, small hobo,
tracks leading off into the horizon
like words along a page.

Somewhere down south
a spatter of shots.
They drop from the sky,
dead splash,
spaniel running into the water.

At a sound,
all heads turn.

Overhead,
the skies quiver with lightning.

CAMELLIAS

1.

In the morning
we find the camellias
tucked in
against the frost,

against
what glitters in the sunshine,
over the barn roof,
on windshields, and
among dried leaves scattered
over the still-green lawn,

baby blankets
wrapped gently
around them.

2.

Yankees—
Our elderly neighbor
shakes her head.
They won't know:

the camellias
might live all winter,
protected against the frost.

She creeps over
under cover of dusk,
swaddling flannel crib blankets
around the bush, tucks in
ducks and bunnies,
Elizabeth's favorite.
Remembers her daughter
dragging it through the kitchen,
sleepy mornings. Stars and moons
and clouds she swaddled her boys in,
And were they ever so tiny?

3.

Years ago,
grown,
one of those boys—

A suicide,
the neighbors tell us.

Pistol to the mouth?

Rope scratching at the neck?

A mouthful of capsules?

No one speaks
of such details.

Not
the sort of thing
you'd ask about
anyway.

4.

In the morning,
petals singed orange
by the frost,
the flowers open,

then open,
then open again,

infinite rose.

Church Skirt

Sarah hangs her church skirt
on the line across the side yard.
Last year she changed her name
to everyone's surprise—Eleanor

had been thrust upon her
by a relative, it seemed.

The tan
to-your-knees
flaps in the breeze
as the sun sets.

By Wednesday night it will be fresh,
full of good country air,
ready to meet
the new
lady pastor.

MOVING DAY

Next door
Edna's adult children
pack the house,

park a trailer
in the front yard
and carry out
what they'll keep.

An appraiser on the way
will likely say it's the land
that's really worth something—

not the house
where they grew,
small boys in their shared bedroom—
but the backyard where,
at ninety-nine, Edna
tended her garden,
bending gingerly
to remove a dandelion
after her evening constitutional.

This year, early winter—
leaves, still green, blanket
the snow-covered lawn.

How heartbroken she would be
to see the house

a student rental,
garage in need of paint,
her rhubarb
gone to seed.

NIGHT IN A PRAIRIE TOWN

Outside, snow gathers itself into corners, sky
inky black overhead,
warm light glowing out from the houses.
Street signs
stand sentinel
along empty roads.

From the center
it's a dense, small town,
but out at the edges
it frays off into prairie,
the moon slung low
over corn
and soy fields.

In the living room, a television
glows out into the darkness,
a muted celebration, bulbs
lighting up the square, the crush
of crowds, streamers, horns.
The ball drops,
and in this room, one year
rolls over into the next,
the small party
glowing out into the night.

A block off Main Street,
a train blows its whistle,
long, lonely cry
from prairie town
to prairie town,
and in houses on every street,
children shift in their beds,
the train's whistle
becoming part of the dreams
they will forget by morning.

Thaw

How good it feels
after the winter's long, hard freeze
to step out onto the snow
and feel it give way beneath you,
compacting under boots, crunching
with the promise
that soon it will be slush
soon water
then mud
then spring.

How good to see
that the gutters
have survived another long winter
of icicles clinging, determined
to drag them down with their weight.

How good
to see rivulets of water
all around, this dripping,
this constant movement,
a call back to life—
into the earth
and out again.

How good the gentle pizzicato
of water down the drain pipes,
storm windows
rattling in the early spring wind.

Diligent Minnesota men
in their flannels
shovel even this slush
clearing sidewalks and driveways
in the afternoon's sun
lest it turn back to ice
once the sun sets, the
cyclical alchemy of a spring
not certain it's ready to stay.

III. FOUND

FEME SOLE

First I knew her by her clothes:
small dress hung in the closet,
suitcase tucked neatly under the bed.

At night,
we spoke in hushed whispers
of love,
hoarse voices
soothed by this collusion. The wind

blew the curtain in,
floating upon air.
Outside, an owl's call.

Her shoes she kept
arranged under the bed,
a neat line of steps

she might take, down the stairs
and into the night

down the mountain
along the road without a shoulder,
damp leaves
dropping into gullies,

the town below.
In one version
she makes it
safely
there and back.

CYCLING

I could tell them
they're not going to find her outside.
If she's anywhere
she'll be underground
where the earth is cool.

Jonna's mother says this has happened before—
a girl gone missing in July
when the corn's up,
then, come fall,
some old farmer behind his thresher
comes upon her.

Her bike's found along the side of the road
undamaged.
They raise the reward money.
Volunteers comb the field for personal items.
It's a desperate time
when a cry goes up over a water bottle
that may or may not
be hers.

What do you think happened to that girl?
children whisper among themselves.

Along the road,
trees hang overhead.
Evenings, I lap the Little League games on my run,
and every woman I pass
could be her mother,
every man I'm in arm's reach of,
a reason to turn back.

ANNUS MIRABILIS

> "See, I have written you on the
> palms of my hands"
> —Isaiah 49:16

You are alive.

The words cling to the side of the wall,
a statement of desperate belief,
that she might come walking—
and who knew—
out of the rubble,

a year of miracle and wonders.

I will never forget you.

See, I have written you
on the walls of the city.

IV. New Evidence

The Most Beautiful Word in the World

A love
that makes you miserable.
A causeless feeling of guilt.

Altahmam:
Arabic for a deep sadness.

The arrangement of flowers
along an axis.

Isolette

To speak your native language
when everyone else is speaking
Esperanto.

Chrysalis
Saboteur
Cedilla
Concertina wire.

Ilunga: a person who tolerates abuse
only twice.

Saudade: Portuguese for a type
of longing.

A word whose definition is: *a time unlikely to ever occur.*

Or a chronically unlucky person.

Dream dresses?
My Korean student struggles,
searching for the word—
nightgown.

Kickpleat
Slipknot
Lumineria.

Topics for Discussion at Today's Meeting: A Found Poem

1. Ken
2. What Ken doesn't want to do
3. Summary of Roger's conversation with someone else
4. People who are chickenshit
5. Other characteristics of Ken
6. What Ken should do—urging him to do it
7. Reporting what Roger has done
8. Ken's not caring
9. Something that's happened—reason for "firing" Ken
10. What they did last night and why Ken didn't go

Safe Conduct

When you buy the bat for two dollars
at the used sporting goods store
you feel like you've gotten
a tremendous bargain—

bright red paint
on old chipped wood.
You walk down the street
carrying it like a cane.
Tapping at the pavement,
it cracks like melting ice,
and people step out of your way,

though you are still
only a sweet-faced
girl. On the train
no one asks
to share your seat. You begin
to feel powerful,
though the man at the el stop candy store
doesn't notice you.
He is telling a joke whose punch line is
Wait just a goddamn minute.

The ladies in the dress shop
you stop into
can't help but stare, imagining
you wielding the bat, fleeing
with armloads of sundresses.

Walking home,
a friend heading toward you on the street,
you hide it behind your back. She
will be delighted, you think. Red paint

bright as fresh blood.

Author Photos

1.
What's with these poets?

Really,
does it never occur to them

to buy a blow-dryer
or a bottle of conditioner?

2.
That guy—
that guy I could tell you stories about. Hands
up under the skirts of the undergrads
who flank him
at the dinner before his reading.

He's a lech,
sure, the men guffaw,
but you've got to admire
his ability to multitask.

3.
This one,
check it out—
she's all,
Look at me.
I'm Sherlock Holmes.

4.
After only three beers
this guy
likes to tell you

he's the twelfth-best
postcolonial scholar in the country.

5.
Oh give me a break.

Of course he has a beard.

LAST OF THE MOGULS

It hardly seemed possible:
     Every year's weather worse
     than the year before.

The talk is of betrayal
though that is likely to be an exaggeration.
Sometimes, though,
the impression is accurate.
     The hungriest bits of the country
     are where nothing grows.

Almost everything is slower,
less reliable
or more expensive.
"It's shit, the situation in Yemen.
Shit," he says.
     The second argument is more subtle:

We could spend another decade in this limbo.
There could be further revelations.
But these days
the suits are firmly in control.

The two crises have parallels:
     a beer-bellied historian
     and a lover of Cicero.

Though what can be done
with such knowledge
is unclear.
Various remedies are proposed:

with some rogues
it is vital to have "a stick in the cupboard"
—a useful warning.

Yet other tricky questions remain.
Only small numbers of nomads live—
an economy as centralized as it is corrupt.

And what of the future?
She took just a moment
to climb up on the Cabinet table,
so beautifully set,
and dance:

Italians can move quickly when the need arises.

Salve Regina

Mother of mercy,
of ten cent candy,
itch cream,
and bee-sting
ointment,

she is the queen
of Gordono's
Grocery and Pharmacy,
presiding over the counter
eight to four.

The poor banished children
of Mrs. Saxman
hang on the bench outside.
Riding around
on the bike they share
they holler at each other: *It's my turn!*
Get off that you God-forsaken child!

To Regina
they spill their change
on her counter, asking:
What can we get for this?

To Regina
they spill their tears

and she turns her eyes—
shadowed in bright blue
—to them with mercy.

She knows all about their mother.

Sometimes
after watching the amount of candy they consume on any
          given day,
she slips them each
a piece of fruit
and says a small prayer
that old Mr. Gordono
won't count it missing.

At four
Ricardo comes around for her,

and the Saxman children
watch as she slides into his tricked-out ride.

She has a special
smooth way of getting into that car
that they try to imitate.

At four
she fades into the sunset
their life
their sweetness
their hope.

SLEIGHT OF HAND

Dinner party, two
judgmental biddies
looking on, clucking
like hens, he—behind you
—rests his hand
on the small of your back,

a touch
that would no longer
register were it
your husband's.

Ten years
of hands
resting on hips,
of arms
flung over one another
in sleep
dulls the senses.
But again,

something
about being
caught, about
being judged,
and then
thinking—
Chuck it all. In the pantry

you press your bodies close,
melt into each other one
another one
another one another.

V. Alternate Endings

Bad Party

And when he begins to hate her—
ears up.
You
should watch your back.
Feigned hatred
as equal a passion
as real love,
as fingers left lingering,
eyes moving slowly over skin
smooth as fine paper.

And when everyone around him
begins settling down in droves,
what's left for him
but to comment on their early departures from parties,
to imagine their sweatpants and sleepy-eyed life,
and to say
it's none of that
for him.

At a party of ten
it's hard to lay low.
Obvious when,
as you come through the door,
you get the back of the head on the downbeat

and the new folks saying,
It's like two separate parties. Well,
you think of telling them,
*Sometimes the folks who aren't speaking
are the ones who know each other best.*

BLUE CITY

i.

The rain sizzled on streets,
under cars,
the weary exhaust of a bus.
Some letters,
a photo.
I walked the revetment stones along the lake,
heard secrets
and kept them.

On the bus at night
high rises loomed.
I looked into lit-up rooms,
curtains left open,
chandeliers, and
space.

ii.

The lake froze slowly.
I walked, scarf
up to my eyes
and tried to remember
how I'd come to be here.

Knew it came
from feeling covered over,
that cloudy feeling

and the need to make it back to the surface
for air.

The city was dark that year.
Something to be said
for frightening yourself.

iii.

The train pulled me through the city
and under it

and I stared ahead.

iv.

The bus
on the inner drive
is too slow.
It stops
every other block
for miles,
but I ride it one night, anyway:

Golden penthouse windows—
1960s bachelor pads
with room underneath to park,

north through Uptown
with its old-age homes,

and when we make the sharp left curve
at Madonna de la Strada
I know I am close to the end.

v.

February came,
and though it froze outside,
blustered and snowed,
the skies had cleared away,
and I could breathe again.

vi.

In the Belmont, I ride the elevator to the top,
to the empty ballroom,
and though any moment now
I could be discovered,
I watch the lake coming back to life

slowly and inside me,
the great thaw.

THE WORST MONTH OF THE YEAR

In February
everything's a mess.
I'm writing love letters
of reconciliation.
One man's sending me music
that'll woo me better
than he ever did.

And I'm falling for it.
Sitting up nights
following the waft of these songs
like a hungry cartoon animal.

And as for you? Well,
I'm planning out ahead of time
what I will say.
I'm planning the end of things
and also a beginning
where you beg forgiveness,
or I do,
and either way
I'm happy.

AGAIN,

we are sorry we fought.
Your plane
rises safely into the buoyant air
and my bed
is empty
when I return home
without you.

Maybe next year
we will have a small house
and a dog we are trying to train
not to leave us,

and by then I will have learned
to take you for granted.

CHINATOWN

The rain spills down over the car's windshield
blurring the red and green pagodas
like a kaleidoscope. The four of us
still damp from the mad dash
from Comiskey
to the car.
The radio on,
we listen to this
and the thunder.

You decide
you can't hold it anymore,
jump out and piss
under the el tracks—
Wentworth and Cermack.
Your friend thinks it's let up enough
to run for the Moon Palace,
so the two of you take off,
leaving us girls
behind, darting
from awning
to awning
losing our sandals
along the way.

At the restaurant
we order Dinner for Four,
and under the table
you don't run your hand
along my leg anymore.

I sleep on the drive home,
wake here and there, a billboard,
the back of your head,
the white-red lights of the passing cars,

and tonight
you are not a lot to live on.

Factors That Control Weathering

In the yard, you rush at me,
the grass wet from the snow
that melted the day before.

When I fake left, ball
tucked under my arm,
you see it coming,
this collision,
and catch me

before I fall, my body suspended
for an instant above the earth.
Stability depends upon

how likely it is
that something will change.
And the rate of erosion

depends upon the environment.
Always, I am afraid

of missing something better.
You tell me to try holding my breath.
Olivenes to pyroxenes to micas to quartz.

This is the direction of weathering.

Wait before responding to letters,

a cooling period
that brings us toward winter.

COLUMBUS EVADES AMERICA

Find a lover you have never loved.
Regret this.
Write about it for years.
Meet him when you are eighteen,
and still think of him when you are thirty-four.
Throw a party.
Plan ahead of time how you will look
and how he will look at you when you come to the door.
Don't plan what you will do
when he presses into you at the top of the stairs
hours into the party.
Rely on your good sense to conduct you then.
Be the kind of person
who *thinks* about things
but never *does* them. Always
think of consequence.
Phone him,
and when he asks you to come over,
to act for once in your life,
let your body be in charge of changing your clothes
and putting on your shoes. Do not
let your head be involved
or you will find yourself on the floor,
shoelaces tangled in your hand,
thinking again,
imagining yourself there with him
and all the consequence attached to it
without ever going.
You will avoid the idea for hours
until he calls back and tells you
he is not surprised.
He was right about you,
but this is nothing new.
He has known you for years.
And he does not think of it
as a victory.

THE RIGHT TRACK

You've begun to regret everyone pairing off around you,
so you think of some woman in the future
but lie alone in your bed,
and I tell you:

You're not on the right track to getting that.

How can you say that
when you're going back to him
and I have no one?

But you don't really say it.

It's the way you stay

but stop talking
after that.

And later,
in the way you leave
suddenly
after more
not talking

both of us saying
nothing.

I hold my breath,
rest my head on the window after you go.

I have been doing this for years.
You've no idea what it was like here this summer.
It was about to happen.

Everything
was about to happen.

"Flight" was inspired by imagery from the documentary *Winged Migration*.

The opening line of "Annus Mirabilis," "You are alive," is after graffiti on a wall near the ruins of the World Trade Center in the days following September 11, 2001. A choral piece based on "Annus Mirabilis," composed by Alex Burtzos, and performed by the University of Central Florida Chamber Choir, premiered in April 2019 at UCF Celebrates the Arts. A recording of the performance and information about this collaboration is available at chrissykolaya.com/books/other-possible-lives/

The following text from "The Most Beautiful Word in the World" comes from the article "Wigscratchingly Tricky" published in the June 10, 2004 issue of *The Economist*: "to speak your native language when everyone else is speaking Esperanto," "a person who tolerates abuse only twice," and "a chronically unlucky person."

The text of "Topics for Discussion at Today's Meeting: A Found Poem" was discovered written on a whiteboard in a classroom in Indiana University's Ballantine Hall.

"Last of the Moguls" is a collage poem built using text from the July 23, 2011 issue of *The Economist*.

"Salve Regina" riffs on the text of the Catholic hymn of Marian devotion by the same title.

Acknowledgements

Thank you to the following journals and publications for making a home for many of the poems in this book:

An excerpt from "Blue City" first appeared in *Flurry*, winter 2010.

"Topics for Discussion at Today's Meeting: A Found Poem" first appeared in *Naked on the Roads: Six Poems*, June 2013.

"Driving at Night," "Chinatown," and "Again" first appeared in *The Wolf Skin*, June 2014.

"The House Sitters" first appeared in *Nimrod* Fall/Winter 2018.

"The Most Beautiful Word in the World" and "Columbus Evades America" first appeared in *Signs: the University of Canberra Vice-Chancellor's International Poetry Prize 2018 longlist anthology*.

I'm grateful to the University of Minnesota's Imagine Fund for support of this project.

Thank you to Michael Eble for the cover image, "Southern Light." You can learn more about his work at michaeleble.com.

Thank you to Broadstone Books for giving this book—and my first—a home in the world.

ABOUT THE AUTHOR

Chrissy Kolaya is a poet and fiction writer, author of *Charmed Particles*: a novel and *Any Anxious Body*: poems. Her work has been included in a number of literary journals and anthologies. She teaches creative writing at the University of Central Florida. You can learn more about her work at chrissykolaya.com.